T0365151

Getting Here

A Collection of Poems by Thomas A. Thomas

Dedicated to all who have helped in the journey, and to Shaun, the end of my journeying.

Order this book online at www.trafford.com
or email orders@trafford.com

Most Trafford titles are also available at major online book retailers.

Print information available on the last page.

ISBN: 978-1-4120-5292-4 (sc)
ISBN: 978-1-4122-3387-3 (e)

Trafford rev. 02/17/2022

 www.trafford.com

North America & international
toll-free: 844-688-6899 (USA & Canada)
fax: 812 355 4082

I. Speculations and Observations

II. Transformations, Loss

III. Personae, Fragmentary Visions

IV. Now

V. Then (Juvenilia)

Speculations and Observations

Horse Dreams

Because my mother rides over
the night hills of this farm,
rides a horse too willing to run
among dark trees, a horse which calls
down to the horse my brother
has dreamed of again, and now stands near,
this horse cannot be ridden,
snorts, trots back and forth, answering
our mother's, presses against the shuddering
rails of his confinement.
The horse dreams of poets running.

In the North, a new Ice Age begins
with rumors of a race of white horses.
Rains follow one another down
the western mountains, across the Great Plains
too often; the air is too cool.
Farmer, you swear at these rains that
follow each other, day on day drowning
the seed they caused to be so late planted.
You protest the coolness,
forget all four directions, walking
on the earth as if you own it.

Or it's hot and no clouds
shade July's burned grass, the cracking
earth; even at night, horses
seek shelter: pintos and roans
stand in tree shadows under the full moon.

In Illinois, women are everywhere talking:
so many horses dying on the highways!
They know the ocean fog washing up
against California's mountains
and staying week after week
has something to do with it. And the men say
California horses are forty feet tall.

1

Now August is cool and horses rush through
the ground fog all night.
Poets are disorganized, cannot stop the winter.
When they see the north horizon turned white
with horses running south, they know the horses
will be four hundred feet tall at the shoulder
and will freeze with stones in their manes
as their shoulders touch. A power moves
in the poets' hair; this power draws down
the leaves from trees.
In the sky between a poet's fingers, glaciers;
at night, women with horses' eyes
leap from the fingertips.

An old question

Is this the moment I can begin
to describe a moment under
October sky in August? Or need I
tell you I dreamed erotic dreams
of body surfing on clear,
blue-green waves and found that
one curve that led to the shore?

And what of the dead dog yesterday,
in its black plastic bag on the
rainy walk? Is that a part of this?
Are you interested?

I am sitting under this October sky
in early August, leaning against
the brick west wall of some building
next to this parking lot, facing a
late afternoon sun; the shadows are
sharp and dense as in winter.

I begin: moths mocked leaf flight,
tumbling brownly down through shadow
and sunlight toward the woods floor
as quick crickets slowed toward sunset.

No, I am sitting in this parking lot,
which suits my mood, under an October
sky on this sunny day in August.
A black pebble lies, barely visible,
like a heart in the shadow of a
white stone.

Blue-green waves collapse toward this
shore in a moment of shadow watching
on a cool August day; I scratch my head,
as does the dragonfly on my shoulder,
in this warmth, where there is no pause.

3

Yellow is not my favorite color

Yellow leaves twirl down outside my window.

Looking down, I see leaves caught in an updraft
rise toward the window, coalesce into a small
yellow dog. It catches its paws on the window frame,
pulls itself through, lands quietly on my ceiling.

The yellow dog runs from corner to corner, never
leaving the ceiling. It sniffs last at the door, looks
down at me until I open the door. It jumps out over
the doorframe, runs down the ceiling above the stairs.

Five minutes later, it's come through the window again.
The same thing happens all over, but this time
I push the window closed, so when he comes back
the third time, he whines, then drifts past, upward.

I cook dinner, watch television, go to bed.
Sometime after midnight, the window rumbles up
and a yellow horse sticks its head in. Its left eye
is brown, but the right eye is turned up, white.

A bit of blue iris shows at the top of this eye, which
seems to be looking through its head, past the spaces
where its ears should be, to somewhere, at something,
behind it. Thus isn't so bad: I may still be dreaming.

But then the horse tries to get in bed, kneeling
at first, then trying to roll in, its weight sliding me
toward its head. When I call the name of the blond woman
beside me, she wakes up, seems to see the horse.

Yellow leaves blow off the roof; yellow horse is gone.

The day's journey: a catalog

In woods: webs
so fine
held
one color;
visible
only
as strand
of
color.

In field: feathers
of a crow
among
cornstalks,
moving in
breeze.

In river: yellow
stick, blue
stick,
circling
whirlpool.

In kennel: sun
in metal
bowl,
shining
among leaves.

Inside bus station: red
roses
printed
on black
umbrella.

Out bus window: boy
flying
kite,
late

for
supper.

Above boy: nighthawks,
red light
on
wings.

Along road: ditch
containing
red car.

On car hood: arm
sleeps,
quietly
pale.

Next bus station: night;
woman
saying, By
rights,
should have
red purse.

In restaurant: woman
forgot
snapshot of
Grandmother.

Behind Grandmother: tree,
leaves like
human
faces.

Above tree: yellow
moon.

In bus seats: sleeping
cats, which
are let
to lie.

Leaving bus: moonlit
valley;
silver bands
move up
and down
grass
spears.

In darkness: sand
path
leads
toward
mountains.

Mountains: black
stone, white
ice: twist
under
quick clouds,
moon.

Left of path: black
granite, low
building; museum
of anthropology.

In glass office: black
man; contemporary
suit and
shoes.

Watching: television
facing
corridor
window.

On screen: speech
just finished.

Man in uniform: smiles.

This is not a motorcycle poem

The engine shrieks;
the motorcycle leaps under me
with the road, me
in the dark behind the headlight, lit
my eyes, by the instruments,
rising the road, then dropping, race
through warm air, now cool,
again warm, now full
with ground fog and the smell
of sweet clover:

The moon rises, and the fog silver;
the horizon loses itself in this light.
Cornfields turn fast, wheel
the flowers, white flowers,
heaped up along the road;
wheel the trees; I stop.
Against the moon, trees
begin to murmur.
Birds cry out darkness, and frogs
spin shrill symphonies
across the valley; dogs
shift in their sleep, wake growling.
Owls turn and strike one another
in the darkness above the mist;
a murderer walks, hands in pockets,
feels his thighs pump,
smiles to himself.

On the ground under me
lie my shadows;
the skeleton, my bones, stand
before me, facing me.
I smile; I have grown used to him,
I kick the engine over;
all the voices rise.
I should hurry,
will know where; the trees

rise around me.
The road grows black,
and the dew like stars:

Now it begins; the dew gleams red.
Under a bridge; a tunnel;
the headlight goes out, sound of the engine
echoes, pounds at me; I aim for the end:
the sky, the mist washes red.
I am out of the tunnel now,
and around the moon, circles of flame;
'round the red moon, fire.

The red fog blackens trees,
rolls around them
until they moan; unseen birds
fly shouting frog symphonies;
dogs drop out of the trees;
frogs and owls heap up in the ditches;
the old man standing under a tree
lets bats circle out from under his coat;

the earth bends away;
all sound fades;
low clouds blur across the blood moon,
and the wind finds my stiff, open mouth
on a hill, and makes it howl.

In the red land, running

An hour before dawn and I am sweating.

Slept under a tree last night, under exposed roots;
dreamed of a silver coyote and his necklace
of eyeballs and blue stones.

Roll down the bank; splash green water in my face;
soak my hair in almost stagnant river: stand in a silence
only I have interrupted.

Eastward, blue gray sky tints red; huge semi-circle
precedes the dull disc of the sun.

Across riverbed, horses stand still, heads down;
above them, crows pace branches sideways.

Two owls hunt late, turn toward me past a cottonwood
at the bend downstream; land, scattering crows
which fly toward low ridge: sunlight halfway down
toward valley floor.

Stare easily at the fully risen sun; red fogs spread
over hills, fields, to the horizon. Months: the sun
still hot as if the sky was blue.

Northwest; upstream; water snake cannibals, queen snake
vines; mud turtle shells dry on the banks.

Run: stones rattle; stumble; sun still dim enough
to watch, past mid morning.

Near noon, sun barely yellow, sky all yellow; the air
thick in my lungs; hear people, avoid them. After noon:
sun dims; orange, red, around three o'clock. I think
it might be three.

A farm; overgrown cornfield hardly green in red light;
cow skin around dried bones; flies, flies, flies:
no one home.

Northwest: maybe cooler; no worse. Red lights in fogs
rising near sunset.

A man singeing hair off raccoon; roast it whole;
it's been a long time; he's headed east.

Road goes north: good enough. Eyeless horse lies
across fence rail. Night nearing; must find place.
Next week, hope moon bright enough: travel at night.

Night Vision

In night I stand
behind a wrought-iron fence;
the sky turns no stars.
In the distance through the darkness
a city floats: a cloud of embers.

Here stands a streetlight, black post
within the yellow circle of its own
defining light.

The roads begin in the shadows,
one from left, one from right, the other
from straight ahead. Nothing moves,

until a classic black Rolls
chrome flashing appears
at the edge of the circle,
its headlights off, rushing silently
toward the pole, which it

hits, which does not give,
and there is sound; there is
screaming, as the car smashes slowly
and the sound surrounds me,
drowns me.

Notes, filed under silence

1.   Late night and snowing,
          I am in my car between
          New York and Detroit, sleeping
          on the front seat, parked
          beside the interstate, alone.
          I wake up: you are in the back seat
          writing on a legal pad, compiling
          "lost thoughts" and filing them
          under silence...

2.   You tell me, "Silence is rarer
          than death." Usually this
          sandstone amphitheater hisses
          sounds of waterfall pouring down
          into green bowl, sandstone pool,
          source of the water's path
          toward river... and birds, frogs,
          insects echo songs among blank
          canyon walls. Now it is dry
          except for a few puddles where
          carp float like koi; a turtle
          sinks into algae-obscured depths.

3.   Another feather falls in the ashes:
          the pigeon, out of reach above
          the fireplace grate, struggles, rests.

4.   It is yellow spring; I follow
          an un-named prairie creek
          toward a stand of mulberry trees.
          A clump of grass slides down
          the short mud bank, sinks
          quietly in warm, silty water.

5.   A late maple leaf ticks on
          its damp black branch
          this gray day in November.
          I watch the faint smoke line
          of migrating starlings suddenly

coalesce into a spherical cloud,
each bird dot moving in unison as all
flash black, then fade – seen edge on –
and at their center, I see the hawk,
reeling, unable to choose one target
among the many, so far downwind
I cannot hear the cries, but only
watch the urgent semaphore
of a cloud fading, darkening,
blowing south.

Gooseberry Creek

Here,
this is the bridge, where
forty four years ago
the kid said, "Look there,
it's a turtle." and grabbed my neck,
held my head under, thinking
to scare me; and I,
not knowing,
but thinking he
was drowning me, kicked. Later
my mother   (a doctor)
said, "That Stacey boy was in another fight;
this time it looks like he'll lose
his left testicle."

Here,
this stain; can it be the stain Curt Weller,
jumping up, thinking to scare the driver, left
in the wood? The blood dripped from his head,
which was caught by the left, the terrible
silver eye of the grocer's car.
My mother   (a doctor)
didn't sleep that night,
cried the next day, in my hair,
about the piece of Curt's brain
she found on his shoulder.

Here,
this is where I go; back to the water
where
my body remembers; where walking
beside the flood-changed banks
I find the same fossils, same
stone-smoothed driftwood; walk through
the same water into ear-deep pools,
listen to the old underwater clicking,
whether the sounds of fish, crawdads.
or stones shifting downstream,
I don't know.

Mirror Series

Mirror of water,
past midnight;
    I swim out toward
the yellow circle,
    reflection of an
unseen light.

1   The threat of the mirror

All night the mirror in this dark room
has been twisting my face until I now
no longer recognize it as my own;
it is impossible to try to say my poetry;
the dog in the corner howls and laughs.

2   The angel of the mirror

Railroad tracks like mirrors run straight
toward where the sun has set; dust blows
around piles of machine wreckage

Twin fires appear in the air, burn down,
shrink into eyes, the eyes of a woman:
she could kill me, spreads her arms,

The sun is rising in the west and the dust
shivers around her; she smiles, she
draws me toward her.

        I touch her, love her,
        I am traveling down some road
        with sunlit trees all around it

3   An experience in the power of the mirror

Don't move; don't.

I stand in the street;
a car comes up fast;
I spread my arms; it hits me,
and the metal shreds, groaning
around me: pressure on my
fingers, legs, chest, face.

Oil and blood run down my legs;
the side view mirror is unbroken.
I pick it up and cross the street.

4   The need to leave

There are owls in this mirror:
when it is dark, they fly out at me,
screaming like women; I can't stay here.

5   Traveling

I almost cannot see it, the train is so black
as it passes,
its windows mirrors turned inside.

6   Prelude for the mirror

Six men in dark coats, black hats,
walk across the brightening snow,
carrying a coffin like a black mirror,
never quite stumbling, before dawn.

7   The entry into mirror

Water echoes everywhere in this cave;
I float down a still river;
blood runs down black trees; dogs
without heads lie still near heaps
of rotting owls; an old man lies
alone in a cavern, bats motionless
in his mouth, between his ribs.
where the sky is red.

8   Inside

I become a woman
the woman before me;
I run my hands over
our bodies, our faces.
kiss our eyelids,
become this dance

9   Out

I walk alone over green plains
a storm's wind breathes out the sky,
touches me, brings rain, brings
lightning, carries gray clouds,
blue clouds over me; rain in my face
trickles down over my skin: water
fills each footprint. When the sky clears
they become a trail of blue mirrors.

Wouldn't it be nice

Wouldn't it be nice to write about a real woman a woman
who is real whose eyes are not metaphysical eyes and
would not terrify not cause ecstatic visions of pain or
violent visions of ecstasy but the woman who would be
warm whose skin would give my fingers actual sensation
the woman who would breathe real air toward me across
the table in the restaurant which would be just a
restaurant and not a dining place of the soul on which my
immortal secret life depended its fireplace would not be a
stage wherein our demonic earth wizards play out
choreographic games explanatory of any of the depths of
uncertain life and death irrelevancies now wouldn't it be
nice to eat dinner at that restaurant to have dinner on a
table which refused to become an operating table on which
I am to dissect my own body which is cooperating
which is falling apart neatly into organized piles of the
gastrointestinal vascular nervous skeletal precisely scienti-
fically accurate divisions of flesh and spirit it would be
so nice if I could really take you to Chicago with me and the
highway would not become the uroboric earth-encircling
serpent known to the ancient Norse as the "Midthgardth"
serpent of uncertain spelling for which the letters do not
exist on this computer anyway wouldn't a real woman who
was not a deer woman or a leopard with the second look
wouldn't she be a lot more fun wouldn't she heal me and
pull me away from this keyboard before I ran before I lay
down on the wood floor crying tears which are always
forever always only almost real tears

Transformations, Loss

In the apartment

There is an old sink
with two separate faucets;
hot and cold both drip.

The wood floor creaks now,
did not all summer; couch creaks
too. The air is dry.

A fire truck passes
and a Volkswagen follows,
then a Chevrolet.

When the bathtub fills
and the water is turned off,
its faucets drip too.

I lie in the tub,
listening to the drops, watch
my body float, sink.

Far off, through the pipes,
there is the sound of a train
switching track for track.

To a woman

The suddenness of the sunlight
this gray day, almost wakes you:
light breaking yellow over the leaves
spreading over rock spaces, yellow
on the water sliding down
green rock;
yellow again, asking
for the lemon flames to come out
from you, to rise from your shoulders,
from under your dark hair. Still,
they don't come; the air
thickens on your skin, turns blue
and keeps it
from his skin, his teeth.

This spring comes, these four hawks turning
above the suddenness of the clouds.
Sun at their center flashes down
yellow light like pollen on your eyelids;
cloud shadows let free the red horses,
the black bulls of your hair.
Even your fingernails become
the yellow of wheat grains, or of
sunflower petals; so you want
to come outside yourself, outside
that envelope of air, blue as the blood
longing to flow out from your veins, want
to touch these bouquets of trees,
the night fog, the moon,
which comes to you.

Poem in one part

Tonight she is several hours gone back
toward Illinois,
the smell of her still on my hands.

Union Station

Red roses printed on a black umbrella,
the leather handle coming unstitched
around her wrist, thick glasses,
a bun of yellowed hair, an old lady
wanders around Union Station with her
scoliosis, her hearing-aid,
and a single airline bag on a luggage cart.

She is bent, shrunken under the vaulted
stone ceiling, the fecund space of air
alive above her, echoing voices, crowds,
the erotic rustle of clothing; a saxophone
plays somewhere, and a young man pauses
in the hours between his trains,
happens to meet a glance, the silent desire
helplessly opening in a woman's face,
opening as they will fall together, will
open the seashells and roses,
sandalwood and musk of their bodies, and as he,
lingering, will miss his last train home.

On waking up Tuesday
in another strange apartment

My clothes lie
folded on the far side
of the bed; I don't
even know what town this is,
or remember my driving here:

supposed to be at work;
wonder what became of Eric,
if he got home.

Her note says: In case you
wonder, you threw your watch
out the window on I-80.

My watch is gone

Maybe you'd like to call me?
My name is Lisa Marie...
Take my number; leave yours;
o.j. in fridge.

I walk around the block
looking for my car: must
be around here somewhere;
two dollars in my wallet.

Over the radio: Viking has landed;
it was a beautiful day on Mars.

I sleep all day, next to the fan,
ice-water warming on the table,
wake up near sunset.

In my mailbox, an invitation
to a wedding; I remember
I'm supposed to call Cathy,
or was it Tina?

The wren-child dreams

After a twilight storm
it lay on my lawn,
wet feathers plastered
on the pink bag of its body.

I have been sitting here
all night at the kitchen table
and now it is asleep, its trills
softened, distant:

Perhaps it dreams of hawks,
or of hawks of fire, of
confrontations in blind pine
stands on moonless nights.

Now it turns clumsily
in the pink Kleenex nest
I have made, under the one
incandescent breast I have hung
from my white ceiling.

Love poem: winter beginning

Lying here
on my pale gold sheets
with you, brown,
our bodies
flowing each in the other
all the so short night
while the first snow falls
outside, whispers in
the dark west window,
I know there are no words.

Before dawn, the sky clears;
we walk toward the still woods.

At sunrise, a breeze;
snow flakes sift down among
bare trees, prism dust
sparkling under the new sun;
we laugh. A crow settles
among a few short pines.

Confusion blue

Why is it that,
just as I have discovered
the blue shadows of winter trees
are beautiful,
I find my own blue shadow
lying between the two of us
and you must leave, afraid
of this morning, with its
approaching, its dead blue sky?

And this bird which takes half
my room: why are its blue wings
always folded, never spread?

You are a phantom; your fear
of the blue light of pre-dawn sky
gives it away.

You will leave me with my blue
kitchen; you would have
changed things, taken my
blue confusion and predicted it
as any ghost could.

Yet you are warm;
your body has weight in my bed,
is taut when we kiss,
you with your pink lips,
me, with my blue.

Dear Stranger,

You have surprised me at my keyboard,
appear in my bedroom door like
a camera, tracking the room as if you
could determine by its condition
my state of mind. You lie down seductively
on my black bed, curiously expectant,

as the telephone begins to ring downstairs,
and sun first burns through morning fog,
slants light between window frame and shade
to fall on my printer and three hasty
sheets of blank paper lying there, over a
half-typed secret I am not prepared to tell.

Present

I'm walking home & it's late
& cold winter and no one's
come home from the party with me
& it's so cold my breath is
frosting my eyelashes shut almost

when I look up & the just-past
first-quarter moon has a pale
green and lavender ring around
it & (how can this be) the radius
of that circle just happens to be
the apparent distance from moon
to Jupiter; so gold Jupiter is
set in amethyst and jade around
the winter's second moon &

I actually think of you - that you
should've seen it - and my eyes
momentarily thaw themselves & my
child self returns: the one that
walked winters on the earth &
snow in Illinois until his eye-
lashes froze almost shut, him that

you & this atmospheric accident
have somehow helped to be present
& here on this sidewalk, even
after I had thought I'd seen him
long dead & lying frozen
under the exposed roots of some
river's dark & stony bend.

Non-poisonous

Lying empty in bed this naked Sunday,
I think of you & your woman-friend,
you two lady vegetarians and me,
& my languid cock rises and pivots
over my grassy thigh like a
heavy, warm mushroom.

Incantations for a wedding

1. *Talisman*

I chant blue days at the sea;
blue flowers grow bluer
on the red face of a cliff; a cold
blue ocean rolls turquoise stones
in and out of a tall cave mouth,
makes slow music, quiet songs,
songs for giants.

I swim, swim naked, swim naked
in the sea's weed bed. I swim and dive,
embrace deep stones, seek that one
which grants a certain
power of flight. I search, for I have
seen the bones that rise and fall,
skeletal spines rolling in sea swell
near the dim blue horizon, have
seen the fingers turning in salt foam,
know that they are real.

Stone, stone, I have you; stone
beautiful with algae, stone alive,
stone green, stone brown. Stone
let me rise, let my bones become
fiery light, and my flesh wind.
Let me be surrounded by darkness
and become fire; let me burn
and become flight; let me fly out
over the ocean, past sight or smell
of any land. Stone lead me, let me
find the old man, child, woman.

I do fly; I do fly over water,
over the indigo ocean, gazing down;
I fly over the blue ocean shallowing
toward some distant reef, and do find
the giant snakes: mirrored scales
flash blued sunlight from under

now shallow waters, flash my own fire
in my eyes as they writhe, hurrying
where I hope to follow.

2. *The Journey*

Stone, stone, you lose your power
so far from land. I dim, descending
through air, into water, drift
toward ocean floor. Mirrored snakes
twist past me: my images multiply,
whirl among their scales, fade into
the blank blue of watery distance.

I lie, I lie, am lying on a sandbar,
white sandbar lying under
the white sun; the sand surface, only
just beyond ocean's reach, lies
twisted by snake weight.
A naked old man walks grinning
up to me; gobs of lava spatter up
from the sand around us; I look
for someplace to go, but between
this sandbar, and the horizon,
there is only water. Still grinning,
old man motions "stay, rest".

Lava child, I am waiting, sleeping,
waking on this sandbar in the ocean;
the lava hiss rises through my sleep,
and the smell of someone's death.

My chest is burnt, burns: a small
naked girl with black hair, dark
eyes and complexion, pulls her finger
from below my sternum, then points at
her chest, where between stomach
and ribs something moves under
a small lump of skin. This lump
fades to translucent yellow; under

the skin: eyelids; the skin stretches
open. A blue eye opens in her chest,
the pupil a clear black circle;
I fall in, drift through warm water.
She makes a sign, so an eye might grow.

3. *The elusive Bride*

Sky, sky, grow green, grow black;
whirl the wind, whirl the ocean: twin
waterspouts twist around one another,
around me, lifting. Salt spray, seaweed
stings my skin, my eyes. Waterspouts
spin me toward another shore; they are
roaring chromosomes, chromosomes
of a giant. I am tumbled onto a beach
of blue stone, black lava flows,
bits of my skin scattered among seaweed
and jetsam. A high haze browns the dusk,
turns blue the moon. I speak this small
prayer: "Where there is a scar,
let there be an eye."

Hours before dawn, crab rattle wakes me
to cold fog melting salt crystals
around my eyes and wounds, in my hair
and beard. Luminescent whitecaps roll
glowing green all along the shore.
Green fog, blue moon passing among clouds
as I stand, glimpse a woman's face pulled
suddenly behind a pumice boulder.
I search for hours, then sleep again,
remembering her face: a blue eye under
brown hair, a brown eye under blonde hair,
set in a pale round mask, full red lips
parted by a smile, revealing blue teeth.

I awake late morning, move north, the
ocean mirror-still on my left, seaweed
steaming on my right, white boulders

and rotting crates strewn on lava flows
ahead. In the crates I find wheels
of cheese, casks of wine. I make a meal,
watch the shoreline rise, twist, fall
in the heat; red wine drops dry on
the white stone I use for a table.
Dizzied by heat and wine, I move on,
stumbling, cutting my feet.

Blood on the lava flow: my own, and
another's; I follow a path of dried blood,
follow as it freshens on black stones,
blue stones, follow it up the cliffs,
follow this path into cave mouth, where lies
the woman I had seen earlier. She sleeps,
the blood still pulsing from her feet;
these I press until the bleeding lessens
and I too fall down in the cool dark.

4. *Ritual*

Cold rain is driven in the cave mouth;
water begins trickling through our
bed of blue stones, reverberating everywhere;
we awake at the same time, find our feet
healed. With a leap, she is in darkness
and running; somehow my feet follow hers,
carrying me deeper, though my eyes are useless,
further into the cave, though I don't
know why. Finally a breeze, and I find myself
standing next to her under starlight on
a cliff face with no way down, no way up,
above a plain strewn with boulders.
She points down toward the cliff's base,
where I see the reflections of stars;
green-white sparkles of light on the surface
of the still, black water whirl around:
above us, among the stars, their double helix
turns slowly, sparkling, rolling northward.

Dawn reveals the horizon: boulders tumbled
everywhere on a flat blue plane of water,
and far off, set upon pillars, the shining
brown skeletons of two giants: man and woman.

I fall, see only the color blue, feel only
cold rushing air; icy water surrounds me;
I strike stone bottom, push off, rise slowly
toward the surface. Climbing out. I hear
the singing, whether the voices of women
or water, I cannot tell. I make my way north
toward the center of this watery plain, where
lie the skeletons of giants upon pillars,
and bone shadows move over tables of stone,
where people are chanting, placing blue
flowers among rib shadows, and singing.

The woman is here, brown hair braided
with blond as she turns, revealing two
slashes which cross below her sternum;
she embraces me until the others come
to pin me on the altar, then raises
the knife, slashes me as she is slashed;
and blood flies up: red against blue sky,
black against white sun,

We wake on the stone table, her on top.
our wounds dried together, blonde hair on
my right shoulder, brown over my left;
we rise, separate; fresh blood flows
down our legs. Brown ribs shine above us
in the noon sun; a blue flower opens
at the center of the stone.

Another horse vision: the first telling

Up above 7000 feet in the Pecos mountains,
had a fever: colors brightened around me;
I was silence, dreaming horse dreams, woke
delirious in a suffocating tent as mother and
guide poured trout water over coal-hot stones
for steam for my throat and horses pushed
heads in through the tent walls, drooling blue
saliva on my face, staring with eyes variously
black or blank white. A roan grew larger,
its mane trailing down and into my mouth;
I gripped hair and held on, was lifted
toward hair-shattered stars, where horse eyes
sparkled, and - vanishing - left my body
alone, my voice, newly resonant.

The transformation

I am a tree.
My eyes sprout flowers:
bees come to me.

Personae, Fragmentary Visions

Approaching Here

I lie like an 'X' on the desert's plane;
I look out of the long caves
of my eye sockets and see
only the liquid sun, white, a
bubble risen to the center of the sky.
I haven't moved,
haven't been able to move
since this desert.
For amusement
I make the sun cross the sky
slowly or quickly:
yesterday was a fast day,
so today is a slow day.

The motorcycle bucks under me
at the gas station:
I pull out fast
into traffic;
a car horn,
a stop sign,
I look up,
see the sun in a ribbed sky.

I lie like an 'X' on the sand;
I think perhaps there is a tree now,
perhaps there is a stone.
Fast days become a habit:
day, sun, blue sky,
night, stars, black sky,
moon jumps east night after night;
day.

I untie the sleeping bag
on the back of my bike,
roll it out over grassy sand, the shore
of a flooded quarry, cool some wine.
When the wind stops, I kneel
by the still water; perfectly,

I see my reflection, my hair bright
from the sun.

I am lonely;
the tree and the stone are gone.
I am bored;
I call to someone beyond this desert;
he will come.

The road turns under me,
slides. Arms forward,
I have ridden all day, and now
rise and fall on the hills, the night air
now warm, now cool,
drop through layers of ground fog;
cool, warm, I ride.

I feel the cool shadows of my ribs
moving over my backbone;
there is the smell of hot white bones;
he is coming.

Where will I be tomorrow? What
draws me toward the desert...
drives me? Slow down, shift gears:
a semi passing another; noise,
the wind pulls at me.

Did one of my bones move today?
Perhaps the weight of the shadows
hanging down...
Did sand move?

Riding west,
I dream:
black Rolls-Royces rise
out of the plains.

This night turns slowly.
The stars all die before dawn.
The moon rises in ribs of clouds;

my bones assume this color and,
I think, the shape
of another spell.

The grass has gone
to sagebrush; this fades
to Joshua trees and cacti.
My wheel strikes a stone;
I skid off the road, tumbling,
sand in my mouth, stand beside
my stilled bike: all the trees are gone,
and the road.

Today is very slow;
when a vibration of metal shakes my bones,
the still rising bubble, the sun,
almost stops: he is near. How
will he come?
I always call.

My bike stood up, I listen:
I look, smell, feel, knowing
no other way to pick a direction.
A sound of air, neither breeze nor voice:
I start my bike; I lose the sound,
turn the bike off;
the metal pings, cooling.

An answer:
don't my bones start dancing?
they drop, even as they
begin to rise.

The sun almost burns me; my clothes
lie hot on my skin. I walk.

My bones rattle: is it the sun? Or
does he come closer?

Do I see something at the horizon?
Is it white?

I know his feet are on the sand;
come closer.

Sticks or stones? What pulls me?

Come, my white bones lighten.

Moon white bones in the sand, a skull.

Yes dance, yes let me rise.

I touch the bones; here is music.

Here is song; we dance.

I dance: is it me, he, she, I dance with?

I dance my bones become free of one another.

I leap up high into the air with bones.

my bones spiral around him we somersault

we embrace the sun embrace the sun

the sun spews out golden glass
beads all around us on the desert

the moon rises and blue stones
become visible in our footprints.

I have nothing to say

This poem is yours, but you must
look carefully for it:
this poem is there among the rocks
where the gray rain falls
on lichen, moss, and marmot shit.
It is growing there in the marmot shit:
rather, it is the marmot
running down the hill from you.

Walk quietly. It hears you
stumbling clumsily after it.
This poem has little respect for you
because this tundra has no need
you can answer. It was happy
lying in the sun, with the hawks
circling above it. And there you are,
still tracking the marmot which
this poem has already left.

Poem from a child's dream

I was a leaf
moved by tides of winds.

I was a stone
sinking into the earth.

I was a river;
I was flowing muddy among
buildings, through an
empty city; the sun
was white.
A building fell into me
and I was the only sound, the only
movement. And I flowed on.

My water fell down a cliff,
fell down among stones
and blended with the light.
I was sparkling.

My African Postcard

On Ngorongoro
crater, the mountain,
a dead volcano:

when the clouds blew down upon it
and were driven through the tall brown
grass
and the whistlethorn
trees,

when the air became
gray, and bent the blue flowers,

when the clouds made forlorn specters
of dark trees hung heavily with moss,
and the trees distilled moisture
from them, dripping it down
through wind on the pink and yellow
flowers,

when the sun pale cold floated
in the gray, on Ngorongoro,

when the clouds blew thickly down
across it, singing in the trees and the
grass,

the birds were black shadows,
appearing, disappearing,
soaring
in the gray wind.

This morning, tonight, tomorrow

This morning I am inside the magician's house,
and his windows are the eyes of bees: multiple lenses
project blurred images on far walls;
images from outside shift across bookcases,
over vague, angular objects, from focus to focus.

Tonight, as I stand up from the table, something
happens, as if a cloud had blown clear
and the sun - somewhere above and behind my head -
briefly casts my moving shadow on the floor.

Tomorrow I will meet an old woman on the stairs;
she will be coming down from my room above,
will have been busy there, having set it afire.

Sunday Afternoon

I was walking in the second snowfall,
out where my father used to find
our Christmas tree.

By afternoon the sky had grown brighter
and the clouds made the snowflakes
look black.

As I walked, the flakes seemed to fill
the air with darkness; twilight,
and she was leaning over

the body of a man, her black and white
leopard skin coat hanging down
over him.

She looked up, a piece of chest skin
hanging from her teeth. She

smiled at me; she didn't
see it,

my father's service .45 in my hand.
Then she did and started
running,

but I knocked her down with the first
shot, and "For God's sake don't"
but I wouldn't listen

because she tricked me before and I
kept shooting her this time.

Night events leading to a small song

Few stars,
ice clouds high
blur   dizzy speed   blur
half november
moon   beams
dance   flashing searchlights
down sky   over trees, bare hills,
frost   maybe later snow
owl voice   song
owl voice louder,   darker than others
a cloud
gains shape   covers
the moon,   rushes darkness downward
owl shape   wings,   spread a silence
darker, black;
talons pierce
my chest, skewer
my legs,   carry me
bleeding above the boiling silver,
ice clouds   the moon now clear and the
stars now gone in wing beats
that should
thunder   now
descending
through silver ice
mist
to a mountain
where I stand listening
through in-gasped pain,   out-spat blood
to songs sung by women   around me under
me, I know   the rocks   I know
the trees   the prairies   the always
sinking water,   I know   I
know,

sun rises behind clouds, over them
and I am in a park of some sort   thinking
this,

To be said at first snow:

You gray sky
You magic wind
You singing trees call
the snow. You singing call
the snow to fall down
like music   singing
on brown leaves
brown grass   singing
You call
          the snow

Autobiography, the Hunter

Years later, fog all around me,
I pass quietly among dead trees,
over riverbeds of fossils.
I am hunting the fox I saw
far down the valley.
It was nearly dark, but his tail
was like a glowing red shadow,
following the leaping arcs
he made, running through grass
twice his height.

I'm dangerous with this fox skin,
even when I mean well.
I may look the same, but you'd
better not believe it; you should
run for your life, if you don't
feel strong. I might not know
that I am lying, and whether
or not I intend it,
you won't find me pleasant
for very long.
When you lift a pear blossom
in my garden, expect a wasp.

If you wake up in this fog
I've told you about, you might
not like it. I'll be watching
when you walk up to yourself,
having hung nine days in a tree.
If you find yourself like that,
you'd better move quickly
and give up talking. I'll come
running up beside you and we'll be
running together.
We'll be running out of that fog
and then I'll be gone.

But you keep running; you'd better.
When you see that black smoke
rising behind the ridge,
you just keep running.
That rumbling in the ground,
that big volcano over the ridge,
that's me.

I swim with dogs

After midnight,   the moon.
I wake and I
hear them calling;   the moon
grows closer over
the dark trees, the woods; the dogs
are moving; a dog
comes running, gritty, wet through
my yard. I reach for it, touch it,
smell. It goes singing into the trees,
the rocks; the rocks
are moving;   I
move
through this, through
the trees, swaying toward me, bending away,
among rocks which hum the silver
darkness, and the song of the dogs grows.
The dogs are running louder;
running and singing, the dogs
are a sea, their smell a tide upon gently curved
hills and fields, running
to a river: thousands swimming there, touching,
straining, rolling. I roll
with them, bumping against their bodies
in cold water, the
wet stones algae-covered under my feet. I
run, I sing, I
swim with dogs.

The hodag, Saturday night

hodag: (orig. unknown) a
mythical creature, reported
mostly from Wisconsin and
Minnesota; known for its
lateral horns, bulging eyes,
and hooked tail; outstanding
both for its ferocity and its
melancholy

You have seen me: as a wolf among
blue flowers, trotting through red flowers.
I dance and become intoxicated
where the red and blue flowers grow.

I have been in Wisconsin; you have
seen me, the shrike with its mouse,
the dog attacking a child.

You saw me: a man at the Oneida County Fair,
the dark one in the corner of your eye;
you danced with me, recognized
my hunting walk.

You saw me again, later, Red Carpet bar.
You drank a blue drink; at least
it seemed blue. We danced, touching.

Your blue eyes under red-brown hair,
mine black, caught each other, surprised
at our compatible dance; the power
rose in us, I lifted you.

The music became something less
than our dance. We didn't laugh, and we
left the Red Carpet.

You take me home to your golden bed,
have opened the curtains tonight,
attack me equally, blue eyes watching.
We tear skin, eyes like knives.

You think you are stalking me: perhaps
it is a game. Now you are fed, turn away
in your relaxation, forgetting.

My old teeth move over your skin, my teeth
from before you were born, from before
We learned this trick. My teeth sink through
your skin: a kiss.

The red lips of your body open before me,
now, here among the flowers, in silent answer.
I am still hungry in the blue morning,
dancing alone in the sad pastures.

A traveler and his road

No way to remember where the road began,
or why, under mist, the pond here
reflects gravestones like teeth
shining moonlight between
December trees.

> Some gypsies come walking,
> selling tickets for the amazing
> Invisible Juggler, with his Mirrors.

This road is the gift of two sharks
found dead and held in my hands
that first summer at the sea:
those first words I spoke
to myself, that morning in Illinois,
so terrible the curtains
flew out the windows,
the sheets slid off my bed
toward the door.

> "I could tell you the road
> began earlier than that,
> and it would be just as true," a voice
> among stringless mirrors, fading.

The road turns down the mountainside, rushing
for the plains; it is a new road -
there is fresh paint on it.
All day the mist clouds have blown down,
bent the blue flowers,
have dampened my skin as I walked, watching
black birds appear in this tree, disappear
from that.

I walk on into the night; white birds
gleam there, blur into darkness
somewhere else, so many birds the fog
brightens toward silver,
rises and disappears over
treeless mountains.

Out of a mound under an ash tree
grows a woman: she stands there,
her feet still under the ground,
crying blood tears. She tries
wiping them away, but then her skin
comes off in her hands.
She sinks back into the ground,
the red meat of her face staring up:
a spring of blood.

A child sleeps nearby, while the ground
around the spring begins to break up;
water rises around him, lifting him,
carrying him downstream toward
that door where he had stood watching
all night: he had broken the glass
with his fist; there had been no blood.

Sitting on a peak near Big Sur, looking out
over the ocean, toward where the sun will set,
I see the ocean fog - still miles out - moving
like a wall toward the land.
It dims the sun, blows over it, and washes up
against the mountains, lit by the still bright sky
pink, blue, silver. The fog rises up the mountains,
swallowing the whole peak under me, condensing
heavy drops on the dry gold of the grass
in which I am sitting.
A man-shaped patch of clear air comes up to me
and says he is the Invisible Poet.
He tells me I shouldn't stay here at night
and if I want to know the way to the road
I should follow the brook down the mountain.

The next night, there is a full moon;
I come upon a woman who is picking blue flowers
under a tree. When she sees me she screams;
the moon turns black, sky turns white.
In this light, I see the trees reflected
in the puddles along the road have no leaves.

> The woman floats downriver with the child:
> they approach a larger river, wide spring river
> where rocks and water sing together.
> A stone bridge arches the larger river.

All day the road has led me
among sunlit trees; by afternoon
they have faded to brush. The plains
open around me.
There is a river ahead, lined with trees;
a tributary comes up beside the road:
three people - a woman and two men -
are watching an animal drown by the barely
open floodgate.

> It isn't an animal; look closer.
> The woman and the child turn together,
> stiff arms tilting above the water.

I look back upstream; the silty water
clears, remains dark. White limbs gleam,
soft corpse skin under the surface:
many bodies, their bruised faces
blackening in the sun, flesh
floating off sunken bones.

> The hands of children line the shore.
> some still grasping for stones. They
> have been floating down this river before.

In the hospital, the emergency room is green;
no one is here. When I look for a telephone
I find an opossum working its teeth through
the neck skin of another animal...It doesn't die
when I break its back.

> A man stumbles toward the river,
> talking to himself, eyes closed.

Insanity, disease; now many people - survivors -
are searching the river, sorting corpses.

One woman pale blue from so many bruises
sways toward me crying for someone
while her lower lip hangs down,
a bloodless worm on her chin.

       Behind trees, the sun sparkles yellow
       on the darkening river, yellow on the
       pale corpses and blue flowers
       along its still, its unsilent shores.

A straw the drowning man might grasp

Two little girls stand on the littered walk,
apart from the raucous harbor, the steaming crowds,
away in the shade in a small park.

The smaller girl rests her head gently
on the shoulder of the older, crying tears which
trace their ways down the comforting arm.

The one crying is soundless; the voice of the other
intones the sadness of whatever the little one's
loss, and of her own losses, and of the greater losses
to come, with such tender patience and love that
all other sound fades from my ears,
and I have no need for old gods.

The Visitation

Late night, darkened further
after the waning moon had passed
westward into low cloud banks;
I was drawn through woods, toward
the lake's sand shore, pushed off,
alone in my rowboat.

Out there on an abandoned lake
in the autumn night, surrounded
by lightless, uninhabited woods,
I might have waxed lyric,
were that boat a poem, or
were the wavelets that rang
the aluminum hull, verse:

and I might have, could possibly
have joined the sudden abundance
of fish which roiled and leapt
in the spray of their own
erotic dance, communal fever...

Still, that was no poem, and I
was only rowing.

So I ask you now, how is it we
come to be here in this darkness
above the water, drifting downwind,
a strange visitation on this peace?

Old man and me

The old man in front of his sod house:
"This here's maybe the last one. Ain't
nowhere you can look further,
and see less."

He says this winter of cold fogs
"is more 'n a little unusual,"
tells me the second and the last
blue moon he sees
will come this night.

His sod house is suspended in fog,
dew condensed on its rooty surface;
the roots are like hairs, each hanging
one gray drop.

We build up the fire, spit rabbits,
turn them over, over,
speak of the wood cut some fifty-odd miles away
twice every month but July.

He says this night something real special
is due: "I been hangin' around
all these forty-nine years
for no small thing."

Now the cold, the fog roof dropping,
the stars bright above a three foot fog;
blue light gathers
around the newly full moon.

We walk out on the short grass plain;
yellow of the moon brightens toward white:
its blue ring swells over it,
tinting the center last. We stand.

The grass grown tall around us glows
golden red, yes, and the land twists downward

beneath us, revealing a valley, a river
carrying blue
translucent trees.

Blue trees grind along the blue, rooty shore;
branches shatter and horses chuck-chuck their hooves
on the snowy plain of blue light, snort breath clouds
toward the moon. The old man
becomes owl, flying everywhere above the drifting trees:
Whu-whu-hoo   Hoo
Hoo.

Change for nothing

The old man in the shop gives me change
for a purchase I didn't make.

The change is all antique foreign coins
and lustrous American pennies,

Minoan coins worn nearly round by
the many loving hands and nervous thumbs;

perhaps they are signals, indicating
the way here, the journey to be made.

The change is mine for nothing - another sign.
It is a treasure slowly accumulating.

Nightly Leaning

His Mother

A young woman folded her arms over her
swelling belly as she walked in through
the heavy doors of Union Station,
moving in a time different from that
of friends who opened the doors for her,
friends she was leaving.

The moon fell west over the trees,
away from her and the train
clattering east toward New England.
At every station, she went to the door,
listened to the frogs peep and trill:
that is the time she moved in.

She liked her uncle's farm; the frogs
were singing there when Nightly Leaning
came out of her taut body to hear them.
She was as abundant as the farm, listening
to those frogs, to her son's breathing,
while her aunt complained of the bleeding
that would not stop until her pulse was gone,
and the breath sighed out into the night air,
the air full of frog songs.

The Child

The child stood in the warm water of the pond;
he was two, and had already spoken clearly.
Now he was standing, arm outstretched
toward the green-winged beetle he had seen:
first, against the barn's red, then against blue.

The winter he was four, Nightly Leaning found
an angus cow frozen in a stream: the calf
had come half out, its rear legs first,
still hanging in the air above the ice. He pushed
but the calf would not go back in.

The child stood in another winter at six,
among birches where he had found his mother's
grave, near the pond. He stood there trying
to find the outline of the pond, lost under snow,
imagined the frogs quiet as if dead, in cold mud
awaiting the light. In the spring he rode bareback
a big palomino, around and around that pond.

His Great Aunt

The palomino had stumbled and thrown her husband
out in the fields, where he had been tiling.
You could see in her eyes the farm going to ruin.
the barn paint fading to wood, the fence posts
tilting, and the corn crib tilting, east: the winds
came from the west, always from the west.

As they stood at the bus station. Nightly Leaning
remembered a dream he had had: he had stood
in a marsh full of birds, had spoken to a big
gray one he thought was an auk; it scolded him
because it wasn't an auk, but a goose;
Great Aunt had told him of the Icelander,
the one who had shot the last pair, years ago. He
wished she would speak to him now.

Nightly Leaning Goes West

He remembered a night in New Mexico; the bus
slowed going past an accident, enough that he
could see the blue purse lying in the blood;
ahead, a third car had skidded, gone backwards
into the ditch, still burned there.

Great Aunt died in Los Angeles, quietly, the way
she had wanted, at a lookout off Highway 1,
near Zuma. Nightly Leaning worked the seventeenth
of his years at a Coke bottling plant, bought a car,
met some girls.

A Memory

Dallas, he remembered; Dallas in '62, the Dallas
he had driven through, headed east. This image
came: the black man walking past; police sirens
and the man glancing up, turning his head
back down to the sidewalk; two black-uniformed police.
the man on his knees: them standing over him
swinging their polished nightsticks: him lying
on the sidewalk, them driving away.

New York, New York

Outside, the man on 78th dropped his briefcase
and it sprang open, freeing a cloud of papers
in the street; a Skylark swerved through them,
one white sheet sliding like a caressing hand
over the metal skin.

He walked with his girlfriend Saturday mornings:
near a fountain once, their steps got out of
rhythm; her shoulder under his arm seemed to be
bobbing as if they were on the sea.
She was his princess.

She liked another guy too, and she married him.
After some time passed, Nightly Leaning screwed
as many as he could.

The Pigeon

He was just too high; he was fucked up; he
was wasted, when that pigeon landed on his window.
tilted its head down to look in through the
screen. He said that thing flew up to listen
as he sang, to watch him dance, and damned if it
didn't seem like that; this pigeon, purple and white,
hung there on the frame of the ledgeless window
for a fucking half hour, just tilting its head
and acting like it wanted to see everything going

on inside. Then it took off on a breeze, arced
across the street: purple and white reflected
on the windows opposite, here and there.

Nightly Leaning and the Last Princess

She watched the blood run off his knuckles, threads
of red twisting down into the drain, noted bruised
cuts on his back, his cheeks, left him a note
he could read when he was sober.

Dealing

He liked speed; he liked to go fast, too: that
was one of his jokes. Cars, motorcycles, stolen
liquor to minors; however: never juice and downs
in the same deal...too dangerous. Eighty-five,
ninety: three a.m. under northern lights, a girl
hung on behind him; no name, just liked big
bikes and going fast, screwing under the moon, under
northern lights, under him at a quarry, on the sand;
still tripping at dawn, the cellophane road floating
in the red light, robins on all the lines; the bike
seemed to him to fall forward, down toward the horizon;
squad car, braking fast. U-turned behind them:
red lights; left on a country road twisted through
fields, woods: they laughed as the pigs passed,
got naked and snorted coke, lay on a rock in sunlight
under pine shadows; back in town made the big deal,
split for Chi-town; he left her at Palmer House,
found another on Rush St. & they flew to Mexico.

Man with a Knife

Nightly Leaning stood talking in Acapulco: business;
made a mistake. Man who tried it made a mistake, too.
missed his heart, found Nightly Leaning's hands
around his throat.

Two men lay on a beach near Acapulco a day or two,
until some woman found them, still alive.

At a Minor Temple to the Sun in the Yucatan
(Nightly Leaning's Vision)

Red ran like a line around the whole horizon at sunset;
voices crowded in out of the blue pupil of the sky;
images: an Arab at a Cairo casino reached for dice;
a Hindu family arose pre-dawn, speaking quietly; the
subway thundered through rush-hour Tokyo; a man, a
woman lay on some Polynesian beach near noon -
Americans: all people of all the world came out of the sky,
each at their own moments of day or night.

A gold disc grew from the sky's zenith, luminous,
vibrating energy; tiny holes appeared in the disc, still
large enough to pass through in flight. He lay on the stone,
feeling almost cold, projecting himself through the
infinite membrane he saw above him: New Orleans club,
bare bulb over a card table; gold disc; he moved through
another hole: Roxy Theater; Kampala airport near dawn,
wood blades of ceiling fans turning above wood floors;
Serge in Brussels, directing traffic; snow blew down
the high red valley; waves shattered coral along the
Great Barrier reef; he streaked among galaxies, passed
below, above, to the left, the right, among stars;
he stood on a shore life had not yet touched, yellow
sun above him, the barren earth flickering with heat,
stones crusted with salt, behind.

A Beach in Baja

Three people, a woman and two men, walk north, away
from their car, having shot it again and again, and
left it on this beach littered with piles of sea lion
ballast stones, smooth, gleaming in the spout spray
of dozens of whales. In the corner of his eye,
Nightly Leaning sees one breach, leaping into air,
without purpose, flying.

The three follow a ravine up from the beach to silence
after rain in the red desert; sandstone still holds
the blue water; crow calls echo among new blossoms.
Frogs sing in all the low places, near permanent water.

Now

Dear Stranger, Return

I have been preparing myself for you.
I have been opening the scar that protects
the place you might visit.

Inside, there is lightness and darkness,
water and blood,
a multitude of suns, and bodies of the dead,
mountains, oceans, deserts, ice,
an angel and a dark animal.

I have burned sage for you,
and made the house warm,
prayed you will come,
yet fear your approach.

I do not offer simplicity or ease,
sanctuary or escape.

But, dear stranger, I believe this is so:

When the heart is ready, the loved one appears.

Autumn beach

The dune grass burdock sits in
the nest of its shadow on the sand,

seaweed stems blow across the
flat expanses like dried umbilical cords,

dry sand grains are whipped into white
streamers across the wet brown sand,

and the rare East wind also scatters
dune grass seeds like snowflakes,

while I lie on my belly, and begin
tucking them under the warm gray sand,

for their long winter dreaming, toward Spring.

I went out

to check
on the moon's progress
over Orion's head,
and to view its hemlock sketches
on the new snow.

I went out to listen in
on Canada geese conversations
regarding the advance of
ice across the
lake's wide mirror.

I went out so the
widgeons' calls could coax
the white light from my eardrums.

I went out to listen in.

Copalis Prayers

I'm walking at night,
when a breeze sets
grass blades in motion,
writing silent prayers
in the sand;

sparrows,
mice,
and insects have left
the signs of their
pilgrim paths
among the burdocks.

The pearled prayer shawls
of the spiders are hung
everywhere
around the marsh
by moonlight,

and we mingle our
footprints,
mine and yours,
in dune grass
along the sand path
beside the marsh,
a prayer written with our feet,

but, come the slanted sunlight
of morning,
I find only
my own.

Love, awakening

I wake warm & tangled with you
under our tousled covers,
come aware
of your breathing, like
slow waves sinking into sand,
over and over.

I open my eyes to the pre-dawn
wonder of you,
then close them, listening
to my own breathing
entwining
with yours.

From outside our window, a third sighing
curls into my ears.
There is now, here,

your small breath,
my small breath,

and the great breath
of the ocean.

Around us

A beam of full moon light falls through the skylight and
graces our pillows, and our faces,
lights up dust motes in the air, like stars
turning silently above our bed.

Beyond, reflected moonlight silvers the high knotty pine
ceiling
and the knotty pine walls, each knot
you said, a galaxy.

Around us lie our halos of moonlight,
around us drift the dusty stars,
around us turn the galaxies. Outside

as it is inside our beloved bodies,
light stirs the sacred matter, the atoms germinated
and scattered by eons ago exploded, long gone stars.

Then (Juvenilia)

Christmas Present (1971)

I have heard it said that Santa Claus died
in an air conditioning duct just south of Lompoc, California;
They tell me that temporary cease-fires are, at present,
being negotiated
in Cambodia and in Pakistan,
in Egypt and in Ireland,
in Uganda and in Chicago,
        for Christmas,   but it's not likely, ho, ho, ho.
They tell me also that the people in the slums will have
    at least one solid meal this year,
       or that the children will have toys,
         or third hand clothes,
And I have it from reliable sources that this year's
    trees of aluminum and plastic are more natural
       than ever, and even smell like pine!
Somewhere I have heard that for once we should try to love
    one another and that GE light sets for outdoors
     are only $1.67,
They tell me to forget   that next week they all go back
    to the tall and windowed crypts
   to shuffle papers in their sleep, and
        many will starve to death   on Christmas Eve
       and many die from bullets,
You ask me if it isn't worth it
    to be human for awhile,
I think yes,
But I am tired of this year's lower-than-ever Specials
     and of great new gift ideas
     and of ideal Xmas gifts for anyone and everyone,
     tired of $4.97 limited-time-only record album sets
    that capture all the joys of Christmas, and of
       watching men carve the flesh from each other,
   strangers cheating strangers,
And most of all I am tired of wars where nobody is wrong,
   And I am waiting for the everlasting light to shine,
    and for the
peacemakers to be called the children of God or of Buddha
                or of the sun.

Second letter from Viet Nam

not so happy not so
   young not so
   sure not sure at all

there are doubts
there
     are awakenings

there is no third letter.

A Ride

After a rain,
a fast plains thunderstorm,
the road drying off and puddles
flashing sun and sky white and blue
in the gravel beside the highway,
and the cornfields the Illinois landscape,
the treed towns and rivers turning around me,
Then there are cars,
many of them stopped on the highway
and the people getting out and walking
toward a rising
drawbridge,
all of them staring
watching the
STEAMBOAT,
the last one, the
Something Queen
all white and new and looking
like she'd just been launched
and them wishing she had been
and thinking they'd maybe like to take
a ride on her someday forgetting
winter and cities and "our new solitude"
and live on in the easy mellow summer
of the steam organ's music playing
from the stern as she passes down the river
and the organ fades,
the bridge goes down,
they all get back in their cars.

Sun

Sun had smoldered all day in a veiled sky,
had made the old man's dark skin shiny with sweat
as he went about his chores,

trimmed the hedges that needed it a month ago,
mended the fence,
push-mowed the lawn that didn't need it (for the smell
and for the mower's cool snick of steel on steel)
stacked the wood against the tool shed he had always
meant to paint.

Then he was done and went inside his old white house
(some of the gingerbread had fallen away)
for supper, bread and soup,
the bread a little stale, the soup four days old,
took a bath, got dressed,
made iced tea and put no sugar in it,
sat rocking on his porch watching the town go by
and the sun go down,
set the empty glass on the porch rail,
loved the silver sound of the spoon,
noticed that the moon was rising, that the air
was cooler, that the last robin was singing.

The rocking chair creaked as he stood
to go upstairs to sleep,
the reflection of the sunset through the window in his eyes.

The day

I took my son to the top of a mountain
and the air was sweet
     and the sun shone
       (the wind snaked quiet over
           the tall grass bending
         it sliding silver bands up
          and down
              green spears gently,
   and the lake was rippling
light and rippling on the rocks,
      the mountainside)
    and there was no busysound
            no motorsound
        was wind sound a
              hawk thistled away to the sun.

Greek Island Dream

Margarita Rose,

we were lying in the sand
   in the sun,
      the old Greeks behinds us and blue sky,
     blue sea, before us
       in your eyes
        in your hair
          in each other's arms, alone,
        with the sea sounds
         and Delos' winds.

Night Song

Tree sings in night wind.
shadow pressed out flat on frosted grass
by clear moon silent moon
          old moon
I walk
quiet spirit
unseen spirit
magic spirit
          of night
     see lights
     see lights move
     hear sounds
     hear sounds of ancient quiet
far off
     owl makes owl song
     dog makes dog song
I sit
  watch mist come
watch light come
          night go
     feel mist move
     feel world awake

     see sun rise
     red disc sharp in mist
          hear dawn song
               old song.

Printed in the United States
by Baker & Taylor Publisher Services

Printed in the United States
by Baker & Taylor Publisher Services

Portrait of the author by his daughter, Megan Rowland

A number of these poems were included in manuscripts that won Avery and Jules Hopwood awards at the University of Michigan in 1974 (Minor Award) and 1976 (Major Award). Some were published in *Anaesthesia Review* and in *The Periodical Lunch.* Others date back to the author's early days in the cornfields and woods of central Illinois. The newest arise from his adopted land, western Washington, where he has made his home for twenty-four years.

The poems in this book range from lyrical to surrealistic, despairing to sublime. The personae range from the monstrous, to the shamanistic, to the shamelessly in love.

Cover and inside photos by the Author

ISBN 978-1-4120-5292-4

51400

9 781412 052924

ADVICE
FOR THE NEXT GENERATION
Neil R. Amstutz

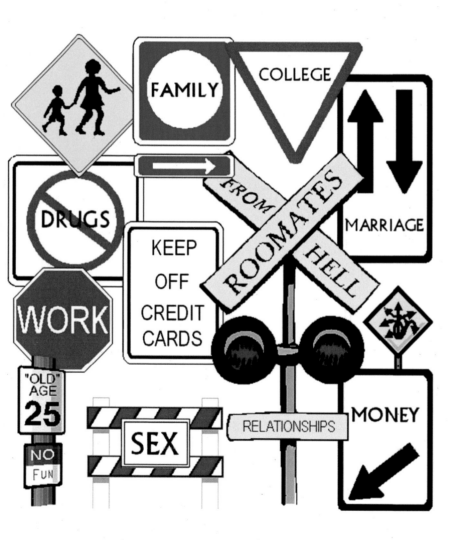